AF211721

GAYLE MIRREL

KINDLE UNLIMITED

The Ultimate Guide on Making Money Using Kindle, Learn The Different Methods and Ways You Can Earn Money Through Kindle Publishing

Descrierea CIP a Bibliotecii Naționale a României
GAYLE MIRREL
    KINDLE UNLIMITED. The Ultimate Guide on Making Money Using Kindle, Learn The Different Methods and Ways You Can Earn Money Through Kindle Publishing / Gayle Mirrel. – Bucharest: Editura My Ebook, 2020
    ISBN

GAYLE MIRREL

KINDLE UNLIMITED

The Ultimate Guide on Making Money Using Kindle, Learn The Different Methods and Ways You Can Earn Money Through Kindle Publishing

My Ebook Publishing House
Bucharest, 2020

CONTENTS

CHAPTER 1

WHY YOU NEED TO CONSIDER
PUBLISHING ON KINDLE

There are a large number of different online methods for making money but publishing books to Kindle is one of the most under-utilized and potentially profitable.

In fact, making money from Kindle is probably one of the best ways to live the 'passive income' dream shared by so many marketers. This is an opportunity to make money while you're sleeping, while you're on holiday, or while you're busy with other tasks.

And it's a chance to sell to a *huge* audience that includes everyone from the tech savvy marketers you're used to selling to, to silver-surfers, stay-at-home Mums, students and everyone in between. In 2010, Amazon announced that e-book sales had surpassed paperback sales on Amazon, which should tell you just what a gigantic market you have to tap into here. This is a far cry from selling a 'make money' ebook via a sales page on your website, which will only appeal to a relatively very small audience.

How much profit can you make? It's massive. Some people are making several hundred thousand dollars a year from Kindle and once they've set that business up, they don't have to do *anything* much to maintain it. Selling books on Kindle *also* makes a fantastic 'side business'. It's a brilliant way to diversify and to give yourself an additional income stream and it's also a great way to make your business more resilient in the face of market changes. You can re-use old materials this way and even use it to promote your other websites, products and other businesses.

Oh and guess what else? It's actually really easy and incredibly scalable. Unlike creating mobile apps or websites, you don't need any particular skills (other than the basic ability to write – though that's negotiable too) and you can have an ebook up and running and for sale on the marketplace in a matter hours.

But there are of course caveats. Making money on Kindle isn't easy if you don't know what you're doing. It's a *very* saturated marketplace with 4.3 million ebooks available in the

US right now, and there are several irritating catches (like the high commission that Amazon charges) that you need to be aware of.

What you really need is some kind of map... Almost like a guidebook that can help you to find your way through the world of Kindle publishing, to avoid the pitfalls and problems along the way and to give yourself the highest chance of success.

And guess what? You've got one! In this book, you will learn:

- How the Kindle ecosystem works and how to thrive in it

- How to create and publish your own books

- How to navigate the (sometimes confusing) taxes, commissions and legal aspects

- How to promote your ebooks

- How to handle reviews

- How to use basic 'SEO' to make your books easily discoverable

- How to price and package your books for optimum sales

- How to create ebooks quickly – even if you don't know how to write

- How to 'future proof' your business against future changes

- How to diversify and appear on other ereaders

Even if you don't have any prior experience making money online, running a blog or creating content, you'll be able to create something quickly and easily and have your own book getting downloads and making money on Kindle within days.

To begin with you might make a few dollars a week but if you follow the advice in the rest of this book, you could potentially be earning thousands in no time!

And the really exciting thing? That will make you a *professional* author and publisher! Are you ready to dive into the world of Kindle publishing?

CHAPTER 2

WHAT IS KINDLE?

Before we go any further, it would probably be a good idea to take a look at exactly *what* the Kindle is and what it's all about.

To that end, Kindle began life as a hardware device from Amazon – though it has grown beyond that now.

History of the Kindle Hardware

History of the Kindle Hardware

The Kindle name was originally the brainchild of branding consultants Michael Cronan and Karin Hibma, while the device itself came from Amazon's Lab 126. The first device was released in 2007 and looked quite different to the ones we know today.

Nevertheless, the original Kindle still set the tone for what we have come to expect from these devices. The main innovation with the Kindle is the 'e-ink display'. This means that the display actually uses real ink, which is arranged on the screen as pixels, just in the same way that regular screens use pixels made of light.

This gives the device a number of unique advantages above and beyond more traditional e- readers. For starters, e-ink displays are matte and non-reflective. This means that they can be read in direct sunlight without any glare or eyestrain. In terms of the way reading a Kindle 'feels', it's actually very similar to reading a real paper book.

Another big advantage of the e-ink display is that it doesn't require any energy to keep on. Once the page has loaded, the ink remains in place with no further power. This means that Kindles can last weeks between charges and that an image can even be displayed when the screen is 'off'.

This made the Kindle a huge hit over other ebooks at the time which could be uncomfortable to read and which would regularly need charging.

On the downside, the e-ink display does have some limitations. One is that it is only available in black and white (for now) which limits the enjoyment of, say, reading comics. Another limitation is that e-ink displays are slow to refresh, which means they can't be used to watch videos or play games. In some ways though this can be viewed as a good thing – it means that the devices will solely be used for their specific purposes. This focussed functionality ensures that people who have Kindles will be using them *for* reading.

Kindle devices vary in terms of their hardware buttons but most use two buttons on either side to facilitate turning the page forward and backwards. Both sides have both buttons to allow for one-handed reading. A d-pad with a selection button in the center is used for selecting menu items and browsing the store, while later models feature a touch-screen for keyboard input and navigation.

Some Kindles now feature back lighting to enable reading in the dark. All of them are designed to be incredibly light and easy to carry around.

Iterations and Models

Originally the Kindle was white in color with a 6 inch display and 250MB of internal storage. This original model also had expandable storage via an SD card slot and was co-designed with Qualcomm to connect to the web via 3G anywhere in the world. This first generation sold only in the US and was later updated with an 'XL' version that increased the screen size.

Kindle 2 hit the stores a little while later and was still white in color, now with 1.4GB of internal memory and a 'text to speech' option for reading music aloud. It was slimmer too and came to international markets as well.

The third generation of Kindle made the device a matte black/charcoal grey which would remain the chosen color. This edition came with a keyboard and was dubbed 'Kindle Keyboard'. It also had an experimental 'browser mode' allowing web browsing up to 50MB per month anywhere in the World.

Kindle 4 did away with the keyboard in 2011, while Kindle Touch also launched with a touchscreen. The fifth generation launched in 2012 with 15% faster page loads. The Kindle Paperwhite meanwhile boated a higher resolution (near XGA at 758x1024) and a built-in LED for night-time reading. The Paperwhite is currently the dominant model is and currently in its third generation. The 'Paperwhite 2015' was released in 2015 (funny that) and has improved ability to display PDF files, allowing users to do things like select text. It also has translation capabilities, a six week battery life (when used for around 30 minutes each day on average) and better formatting capabilities (including a new font called 'Bookerly').

There is also a modern update to the traditional Kindle, the Kindle 7, which was released in 2014. This model is a basic Kindle with a touchscreen and has a 1 GHz CPU. Another modern model is the 'Kindle Voyage' which came out in 2014 with a 6-inch 300ppi e-ink display and an adaptive LED that responds to the lighting in the environment.

Kindle Fire

The Kindle Fire is a more traditional Android tablet that carries the Kindle name. This is a device that looks and feels a lot like your typical Nexus device and which has access to the Amazon App store. That means it can be used not only to read your selection of Kindle books but also to handle a number of other activities whether that means playing Angry Birds or watching YouTube.

Although the three Kindle Fire tablets are Android devices, they have a secondary 'skin' provided by Amazon called 'Fire OS' which makes them look and behave differently.

Unlike other Kindles, there is no 3G option for Kindle Fire and the screen is a regular tablet screen that can produce a fair amount of glare.

The Kindle Store

Perhaps the most important aspect of the Kindle is the Kindle Store. The Kindle Store is basically a marketplace and distribution platform that allows users to browse and purchase ebooks. This works just like an app store, or like the regular Amazon store, in that users search for titles using the usual search box and then just click to buy. Once they do that, the book will then download to their device and they can start reading it from their personal 'library'.

The Kindle Store is actually bigger than that though. For instance, users can also download Kindle apps in order to access their Kindle books on their smartphones. With the Kindle app for Android and iOS, a user can browse their library and read their selection of books. At the same time, they can also browse the store in order to purchase new books. Books on Kindle devices and the app will automatically be synced so that you can stop reading on your Kindle, then pick up from where you left off on your mobile when you're bored in a queue at the bank. This is important for us as publishers, as it means our audience is actually much larger than only the number of people who own Kindles.

Likewise, it's also possible to buy Kindle books through Amazon.com. This way, users elect to buy either the physical or digital version of the book when they're looking through the store. Subsequently, the file will be downloaded to the Kindle or they'll be delivered the hard copy.

Books sold on the Kindle Store are available in ePub format. This format allows for certain additional features such as interactive menus and it helps to keep your books protected.

As on Amazon and most app stores, it's possible for users to leave reviews about the books which can encourage or deter other users from making a purchase. This, as well as factors such as sales and keywords, combine to influence the ranking order of the books for different search strings. This is something we'll be looking at in a lot more detail later in this book.

The Kindle Store has recently introduced a number of initiatives. These include a subscription service called 'Kindle Unlimited' and a rental system that allows users to 'borrow' books. We'll look at what both these mean and whether you should opt in or out later on.

For us, the biggest appeal of the Kindle store is that it's a ready-made distribution platform. If you can get a book to be featured prominently in this platform, then you can guarantee it will be seen daily by hundreds or thousands of people. People can then order the books without you having to lift a finger and they'll be buying with one click, without you having to gain their trust first or manage their transaction.

In this way, a distribution platform becomes a 'route to market' and it makes the whole process of selling considerably easier. Now you don't need to worry about reaching your buyers, gaining their trust or any of those other things. It's like getting a product onto the shelf of a massive store and it's one of the gigantic advantages of being a Kindle publisher.

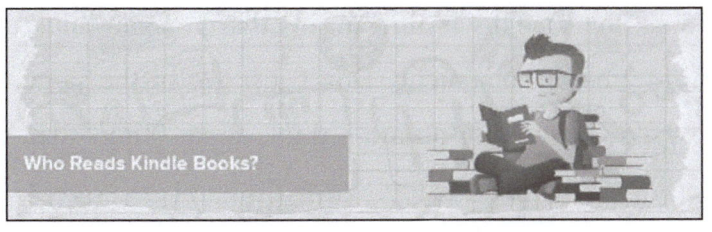

Who Reads Kindle Books?

Who Reads Kindle Books?

Now you know the basics of the Kindle ecosystem, you should start to have a good idea as to how your book will be found, read and enjoyed by other users. What you also need to think about though, is who will be reading your books and when. What is it that makes the Kindle so popular?

Understanding this can help you to better understand your audience and thereby to make more sales.

Of course there are countless types of people who use the Kindle and this is one of its major appeals – the Kindle is a *particularly* user friendly piece of technology. Amazon is such a household name that it's something everyone can trust. This is important because a lot of older web users often worry about security when shopping online and this can prevent sales. At the same time, the Kindle feels a lot more like a book to hold and use and has a very simple and straightforward interface. As such, it is enjoyed by people who might not normally use tablets – a much wider demographic than most digital marketers are used to selling to. This in turn means that you can think a little wider in terms of your niche. Don't just go for the same topics you're used to covering online – think about things that Mums or elderly readers might enjoy.

The main appeal of the Kindle is that it can be easily taken anywhere and can hold so many books. This is the perfect solution if you're going on holiday for instance and you want to read a lot of books without adding too much weight to your luggage. And because Kindles offer 3G anywhere in the world (depending on the model) you can even buy and download new books to read while you're out there.

Holiday makers and travellers then are two of the biggest groups to read on Kindle and many people will dust their devices off mainly when they're going on holiday. Think about this when choosing what type of books to write – if it's something people would typically enjoy on a holiday (like a travel guide) then you might be on to a winner!

Likewise, a lot of commuters will read Kindles as a way to entertain themselves on the train/subway/bus. This again opens up another larger audience for your books: the professional. Think about the kinds of things that city workers might like to read and the kinds of things they're specifically going to be in the mood to read on the way into work.

CHAPTER 3

CHOOSING YOUR NICHE

This brings us on to the first big question you'll need to ask when creating your Kindle book: what niche are you going to try and compete in?

This is actually one of the most important decisions you'll make in the entire process as it will determine the audience for your app, the marketing options available to you, the amount of competition and much more. If you don't choose your niche carefully, then you'll end up making a lot more work for yourself when it comes to promotion and in the worst case scenario, you may even limit the size of your potential audience to such an extent that it's hard to make much money at all.

Let's take a look at how you can ensure you get this bit right...

Why You Can't Choose Any Niche

Why You Can't Choose Any Niche

If you have aspirations to be the next JK Rowling, then you might be tempted to make your book a fiction book. This is of course up to you, but you should know going in that you just made your life a *lot* harder.

You can market your book yourself and we'll look at how that works later on. But in the meantime, if your main aim is to make money then you want it to be possible for people to find your book *without* having heard of it before.

If your book is about gardening, then you can call it *Gardening in Winter*. There's now a very small chance that someone might search for that exact phrase – not even knowing that your book exists – and find your title to download!

But on the other hand, if your book is about wizards and it's called *The Majestic Journey of Mr Darkshadow*… then people aren't likely to search for that title unless they happen to know about your book and they've read lots of good reviews. There are ways you can get around this, but it's not going to be as easy to get discovered.

So making your book something that will get searched for is a good idea. And at the same time, if you can set out to solve a very specific problem, then this is something that will really help you to market yourself and sell your book.

This is why non-fiction books tend to work very well and especially those that solve a simple problem that a specific type of person is looking for. Think about the problem you're going to solve and think about the kephrase that your book is automatically going to lend itself to. Will people search for the title of your book? Will they search for related phrases?

But now you have another question: do you aim for a large audience or a smaller one? Do you create a book that's going to be a 'small fish in a big pond' or do you go where there will be much less competition.

Case in point: you can either create a book about fitness or you can create a book about 'curling' (the sport that involves sweeping ice).

The fitness book is going to have a massive potential audience and in theory, this means that you can sell to a much bigger number of people and make a lot more profit. But on the other hand, that fitness book will also have the challenge of needing to stand out in a *very* crowded market place. In other words: there are going to be hundreds of other ebooks competing with you to make it to the top and your chances of standing out will therefore be quite slim. Things get worse when you consider that some of those publishers are going to be massive corporations with millions of dollars to spend on marketing. You'll be competing with bestselling authors in the niche like Tim Ferriss and Arnold Schwarzenegger and Pavel Tatsouline.

Call your book 'Fitness 101' and you're setting yourself up for failure.

Conversely, when you create a book on curling, you're going to find it much easier to stand out. Post to a curling forum that you've just released a new book on their favorite topic and this will probably be enough to lead to a number of rapid downloads. People will be excited that there's no content on their favorite subject because it's rare that that subject gets tackled. What's more, you have clear places to go to promote yourself: curling forums and Reddit pages for example. There's less content here, so posting will get you noticed. You can probably get coverage in magazines even because the niche is so much smaller and there's less news to report. Try and get coverage by *Men's Health* however and you'll be competing with thousands and thousands of other emails.

You can pay for Google AdWords in the curling niche and get lots of clicks for a relatively low price (because the cost per click is calculated using a bidding process) and even if you do absolutely no marketing and no optimization, your book will automatically probably be on the first few pages of the Kindle Store when someone searches. Why? Because there are probably only a few pages worth of content!

But that's not to say that curling is the perfect niche. Of that small audience of people interested in curling, you're only going to manage to convince a small percentage that they should read your book. As a result, once you saturate that market, you may well end up with no one left to sell to.

Another problem with the curling niche is that you're not going to change anyone's lives. You might be wondering why that would matter but think of it this way…

The reason that most internet marketers choose niches like 'make money online', fitness and dating, is because those niches very genuinely could change someone's life. Being in better shape and feeling more confident as a result, having less body fat, being more successful with the opposite sex and earning more money – these are all things that are highly motivating.

These are universal goals that almost all of us can at least appreciate. And that makes your book much easier to sell.

Better yet, if your book promises to make someone money, then in theory that expense should be an investment. That way, people will happily spend the money because they're going to be more likely to think they'll make it back. This in turn means that they don't see any 'downside' of spending the money on your book!

Choose curling and you won't have this kind of 'life changing power' unless your book happens to be aimed at people who plan on making this their career. While people might still be happy to pay $5 for a book on curling on a whim, you won't be able to charge as much as you could for a book that offered to make them rich and attractive, or that they *need* to advance their career and fulfil their dreams.

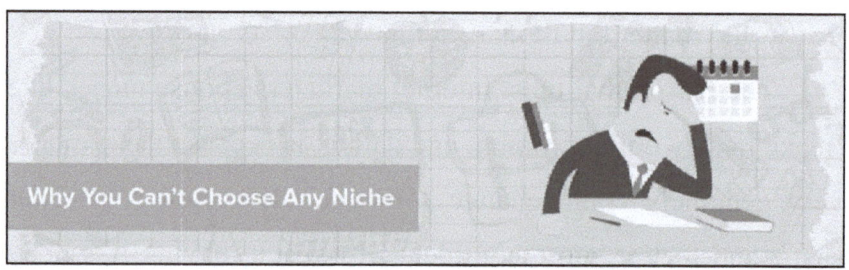

Why You Can't Choose Any Niche

How to Pick the Perfect Niche

The key then is to try and choose a niche that will offer all the benefits of a big category without being so incredibly difficult to stand out and gain traction in. One way you might think about this is to go 'big but not too big'.

A perfect example of this is to choose an industry or a career, and ideally you want something that you know a bit about.

A perfect example of this comes from someone I once knew who wrote a book on 'stage lighting'. Stage lighting is a niche that 99.99% of the population would have absolutely no interest in. However, that remaining .01% of people would actually benefit greatly from some kind of book to help them further their career. That guy managed to get his book mentioned in an industry magazine and on some websites and quickly it became the 'number one' book in that category.

The result? He was making hundreds of dollars a month. On top of his regular salary that was a *very* nice little sum of cash!

Likewise, you might work in a different career that you happen to know a bit about. Or perhaps you can use your internet marketing skills and hone them in on a specific career or subject. For example, how about teaching a counsellor how to set up their own website and promote it online? Or how about doing the exact same thing for personal trainers? For people who want to sell homemade jewellery on Etsy? For people who want a career in photography?

You should of course research the niche that you intend to go into as well. Don't dive straight in *assuming* that there won't be that much competition as this can be a big mistake. Instead, make sure to actually do a few searches and to find out for sure whether or not there are lots of other books there. Likewise, do some research as to the other routes to market you can use to promote yourself.

More Tips for Finding Your Niche

Another tip is to think about the contacts and opportunities that you already have available to you. Almost all of us know people in *some* kind of important position and almost all of us have got some useful contacts or experience.

In other words, if you happen to have been a number one trader for a big firm – then that gives you a lot of reason to write a book about trading. Not *only* are you going to have lots of useful information to bring to the subject (writing what you know is always a good idea) but you're also going to have contacts within your previous organization, with relevant industry magazines etc. that you can use.

Likewise, if you just so happen to be best friends with the editor of *Gardening Monthly*, then that's a very good reason to consider making a book about gardening.

Another option is to approach a large niche but to find your own 'corner' of that niche and your own way to make it your own.

A great example of this would be to write a book about stretching. This is a 'fitness' topic broadly but it's also a topic that is a lot more specific than that. If someone wants to improve their flexibility, then you stand a better chance of getting noticed.

Or how about a sub-category of fitness? That might mean 'metcon' (metabolic conditioning), HIIT (high intensity interval training), the paleo diet (although there's a lot on this topic) or 'power building' (a combined form of bodybuilding and power lifting). You could also look at a particular training appliance ('Guide to the Chest Press') for when people buy new machines to use at home. This is a particularly good option and you can also write 'guides' to other products. For instance, what about a guide to using kitchen knives (rather than a generic book on cooking). This way, you could even speak to sellers of popular knife products and see if they might recommend your book to their buyers if you do likewise. In fact, you could even recommend it yourself in a review of their product...

Instead of writing about martial arts *in general*, how about writing about a specific martial art? Better yet, is if you can land on something that is up and coming. Find a movement that is emerging online and be the first to write about it and your book will be ready for when people get really interested in that subject in their masses.

This once again goes hand in hand with products. For example, how about writing a guide to using the latest iPhone model the moment it comes out? Or how about writing a guide to those hover boards? You can be the first to what is likely to be a big niche in this way and at that point it becomes a little like market speculation!

Or how about choosing a particular audience within a much larger niche. So instead of writing a fitness book aimed at everyone who wants to get fit (i.e. everyone), you could write a fitness book aimed at the elderly, the diabetic or even people who travel a lot. In all these ways, you're finding unique niches that have a broad, universal appeal but also might be easier to rank for in the search results.

But... I Want to Write Fiction!

But… I Want to Write Fiction!

All of this is not to say that you absolutely cannot write a fiction book and be successful. In fact, there are several ways you can have a hit on your hands if you write fiction – you just need to think carefully about how to go about it.

One tip to that end is to think carefully about genre. In this regard, genre is going to work a lot like choosing a niche. Here, you want to pick a subject that will give you lots of marketing options and that will have lots of fans ready to get excited about it and to help you promote it.

For example, if you write a cyber punk book, you'll find that there are whole forums where people discuss the subject and would probably be interested in reading what you've written. Likewise, you can find people who are big fans of gothic horror, or of romance novels. If your book is really good, then word of mouth might be enough to help it spread. You can also use these phrases and words in your description and elsewhere on your listing in order to make your book easier to find.

Likewise, it can help to think about which books are similar to yours. I'm not telling you to copy, or to write books about stories that don't excite you (would I be that cynical?). I'm merely saying that if your book *happens* to have a similarity to *The Da Vinci Code*, then it won't hurt for you to emphasize that connection and to mention it. This way, people will be able to more quickly grasp what your book is about and whether they might like it and again it might be more likely to come up in searches or as a suggested 'similar' book.

CHAPTER 4

CREATING AWESOME BOOKS
THAT WILL SELL

Now you have the niche, the next step is to start creating your book. This is where a lot of people will get put off but even if your English is terrible, I implore you to read on because there are ways around that.

Here's some bad news if your plan was to flood the Kindle store with low quality books: Kindle books need to be *good* if they're going to do well. This is down to the fact that you want to try and get as many positive reviews as possible and as few negative ones. Likewise, it's also down to the fact that readers can very often choose to read a 'free sample' of a book in order to get a taste for it. This means they'll get to see what the quality of the writing is like, whether the subject matter is any interest to them and whether you appear to know what you're talking about.

And if your book is low quality? Then they won't be very likely to order the full thing. Likewise, some textbooks allow students to *rent* the book for a while on a '7-Day free trial'. If you have created an eTextbook for students (an interesting alternative to the career option), then again you need to ensure it's good if you're going to hold their attention for long enough.

What Makes a Good Kindle Book?

So with that in mind, what makes a good Kindle book? And what makes a good book *generally* for that matter?

A good place to start is with the tone and the style of your writing. This needs to be appropriate to the tone of the niche you're writing for. So if your book is about financial modelling, then it's likely to be a more formal style of writing than if your book is about drawing cartoons for example.

But in any case, you need to ensure that your content is engaging, that it is fun to read and that people want to keep on reading through it. A good way to achieve this is by using a narrative structure – i.e., make your book a story. Even if it's a non-fiction topic, that doesn't mean you can't open by talking about your experiences and by leading the reader in gently to the subject.

You need to make sure that your content is well written and that it is going to sound professional. That makes it a very good idea to read through the book yourself and to get friends to read through it as well if possible. You want to get rid of as many typos or grammatical errors as possible. A few are absolutely bound to fall through the net but you need to keep them to an absolute minimum in order to maintain that professional and trustworthy impression. If your book is badly spelled or has lots of errors, then your readers will feel tricked or short changed – and they're unlikely to buy the full book.

Note that Word comes with an in-built spell and grammar checker. Make full use of this! But do bear in mind that it can't replace having a human set of eyes read over your content for you. Another tip is to try reading out loud, which will help you to improve the flow of your book too.

Both these last two points are particularly important for that initial 10% of your book – the free sample and a bit beyond. This is how you'll really engage with your reader and how you'll get them to keep wanting to read more.

Another tip here is to spend a little time talking about what's coming up in the book and setting the scene. This is valuable because it will get your readers excited for what they can learn and what they can expect if they buy the full book. Having a 'what you will learn' at the start of the book is always a good idea, as is teasing some of the most valuable tips and insights you'll be sharing later.

At the same time? Make sure you point out just how your book is going to be different from all the others on the market. Especially if you're going for a big niche – you need to bring something unique and new to the topic that people haven't read before. If it's a book containing workouts then you need to discuss the unusual and little known training methods found in that book that no one else is aware of.

That said though, you don't want to waffle on with so much promise that it looks like you're just padding out the book. Aim to share at least one actionable tip in your intro that will impress your readers so that they will believe they can get more like that by reading your full text.

More Features and Aspects

As well as ensuring that your book is well written and that you're providing real value, you can also improve the impact your book has by thinking about some other aspects.

One important thing to consider for example is the length of your book. Of course longer books will at least *appear* to provide more value, so you need to ensure that your book is long enough to look like it's worth the money you're charging. The longer the book, the higher the price tag you can get away with. Of course though it's not all about the length – there are many other factors that are equally as important such as the value of what you're sharing. Try to ensure that you're ticking both boxes – have a long book that is nevertheless densely packed with useful and actionable information.

A good 'standard' length is 10,000 words. That is long enough that it will feel meaty and won't get complaints. At the same time though, you can probably go down as low as 5,000 words and there's no upper limit in terms of how long you want to make the book. If the mood takes you, you can make your book 50,000 words long! Make sure that you feature that prominently in the description though so that people recognize they're getting extra value. That length is a selling point!

Another consideration is imagery. Remember we discussed earlier that the e-ink display is black and white, meaning that color images might not have quite the same impact as they could do on another platform/in another format. Nevertheless, choosing to have *some* images will help to make your book look more professional and will also make it more engaging.

You also need to think about the font, the layout and various other aspects of your book – though we'll be talking more about the formatting and things later on. Just suffice to say that a large wall of tiny text is *not* an appealing thing to come across when you get a new book to read. On the other hand, if your book is nicely spaced out with large, crisp fonts, lots of images and a welcoming narrative structure that promises lots of interesting value inside… then that becomes a different matter!

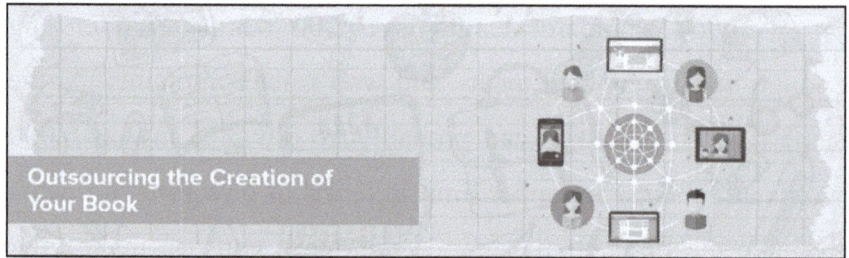
Outsourcing the Creation of Your Book

Outsourcing the Creation of Your Book

Now, some people might be reading this and wondering how on Earth they can possibly write a book that's 5-15,000 words long *and* format it all beautifully. They say that 'everyone has a book in them' but that is not necessarily to say that everyone has the ability to *write* that book and make it entertaining and engaging. So the question then becomes how you're going to write that much content without it absolutely killing you.

Moreover, there's a high chance that *some* people reading this won't speak English as a first language or won't be confident in their ability generally to write in an engaging and entertaining manner. What if you're just *not* a good writer?

In that case, you need to think about outsourcing the creation of your content. You can find writers on freelancing sites like People Per Hour (www.peopleperhour.com), UpWork (www.upwork.com) and Elance (www.elance.com) and you can also find them on 'marketing forums' like Digital Point Forum and Warrior Forum. You can expect to pay anywhere from $1 to $5 per 100 words but do keep in mind that you will get what you pay for: it's worth paying a little bit more and getting a writer who will do their research and make your book sound professional. If you like, then there's nothing stopping you from creating a detailed set of guidelines for them to follow and helping them to see what the layout of your book should be and which key points you want included. That way, they write the book but you can remain the 'director' as it were.

At these kinds of prices, you can create a book for $100 to $500, which in theory you should be able to make back. Of course it's better to start with something you've created yourself but if this is your only option, then it's still a viable model. Normally, you'll find turn around time is very good too – anywhere from a few days to a few weeks.

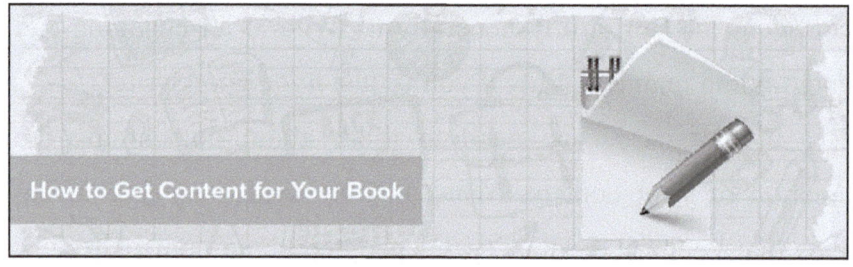

How to Get Content for Your Book

How to Get Content for Your Book

What if you don't want to write the content yourself but you don't want to pay someone to do it either?

Turns out, there are still options open to you! One such option is to create something using content that you already own. This is a particularly viable option if you're a blogger for example. In this case, all you have to do is to select several blog posts you've already written and then write a forward and compile them into a book. Add a couple of 'unique posts' to the book as well and this is something you can even market on your site.

On the web, it's very important that all content be 'unique' as otherwise, Google won't show it. But in the case of an ebook on Kindle, there's no way that Google will see the content and you don't need to rank on Google. As long as the content is *yours* and you won the copyright, there's absolutely nothing stopping you from publishing it on your blog *and* selling it in a book that you've created!

Another option is to try and get other people to write your content for free. This might sound like it wouldn't happen but it can do if you find the right crowd and they're excited at the prospect of being in a book. For example, you could create a poetry anthology and run a competition for people who want to try and get themselves in the anthology. Then just publish those poems and charge a small fee for people to read them. The same goes for short stories.

There are more options too. Depending on your coding prowess for instance, you may be able to write an algorithm that

41

generates certain types of content for you. That might mean writing a program that generates bodyweight workouts for instance, or writing a program that comes up with strange poetry (now there's an interesting project!).

You can even repackage and sell content that is in the public domain. Books that have no copyright any more are fair game and if you can find something that's old but still relevant, this is a viable option.

While all these options are legitimate routes to take though, you'll always have a lot more success if you write your own content specifically for the purpose of selling a book. Remember, people are going to be reading this and you need to impress them with high quality writing and useful information!

Other Platforms

Note as well that this also works *in reverse*. That is to say that there's nothing stopping you from publishing the book you created for Amazon elsewhere and making even more money from it. You can publish to Barnes & Noble, Sony's Nook eBook store, iTunes, Google Play and more – and all of these will help you to get more exposure (this isn't an option if you want to enrol in Kindle Select though unfortunately).

Better yet, why not physically publish your book? POD publishing is 'Print On Demand' publishing and basically means that you can publish a book in a physical format and only pay each time the book is purchased. In other words, you don't need to order 1,000 copies and then try and sell them. Amazon has its own Print On Demand service even (http://www.amazon.co.uk/b?node=4780051031) which you can sue at the same time as selling through Kindle Select. You can then promote this from your website and in videos and it will look *very* professional as you'll have a physical item to brandish! Another option is to use LuLu (www.lulu.com).

Horizontal Distribution

That said, if you're looking for a way to increase the volume of content you can create, or you're looking for a way to maximize your potential income, then another option is to take the 'horizontal distribution' approach. This has a real danger of being spammy, so do be careful here but it's worth a consideration.

Horizontal distribution effectively means that you're taking an idea for a book or a service and then you're marketing that to a wide audience under several different guises with mild tweaks.

For example, if you took the suggestion earlier of creating a book that provides SEO and internet marketing advice for people in particular careers (how to promote your counselling business online), then you can always repackage a lot of that same content for different businesses.

Simply write a forward that is specific to the particular niche that you're looking for and then write a generic book on how to set up a website, how to market yourself with SEO and how to set up an online order form/email marketing list *etc*.

Now, each time you mention something that relates *specifically* to the certain niche you're interested in, just include a small tag [SPECIFIC]. Now you can search for that [SPECIFIC] tag and simply change the relevant text to relate specifically to your given niche. 90% of your book might use the same content but you can now sell it as:

- Online Marketing for Counsellors
- Online Marketing for Personal Trainers
- How to Market Your Web Design Business Online
- How to Market Your Jewelry Business Online Ad nauseum...

Nobody is going to try and buy more than one of these books as the areas of interest are so diverse – so you're not cheating anyone out of a high quality purchase. At the same time though, you'll find that you're able to get clicks from many different niches and thereby improve your exposure significantly. This is what is meant by 'horizontal exposure' because you're spreading your product out horizontally for lots of people to find.

Likewise, you might be able to recycle specific elements from particular books. So if you have a book on workout out while travelling and a book on working out for students, you could perhaps recycle the chapter that details specific bodyweight workouts and diet tips.

It's up to you if you want to go this route or not but just note that you can create a lot more products a lot more quickly this way. And if you have 1,000 books in the store, then it doesn't matter if you only sell one of each a week… that's still going to be thousands of dollars' worth of profit. Ultimately, if you can increase the volume you're putting out, then you can scale your business infinitely and that results in a near fool-proof way to make money.

CHAPTER 5

FORMATTING YOUR BOOK

Okay, now you have your niche, you've written your book and you know who its aimed at. The next question is how you go about turning it into an actual *Kindle* book. The good news is that this process is quite simple – though there are some things you need to keep in mind. You need to ensure that your book is going to conform to industry standards, that it is going to look good on Kindle and that it's going to behave the way that your audience expects it to.

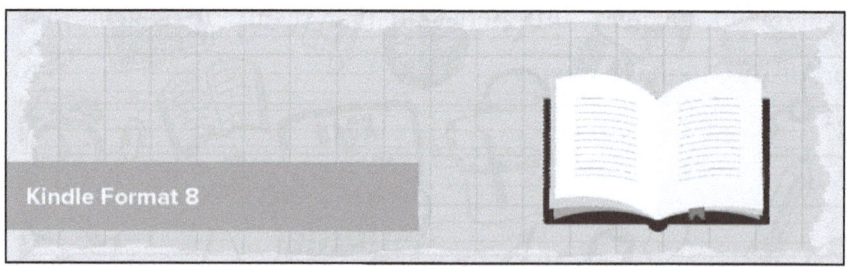

Kindle Format 8

Specifically, you should aim to stick to Amazon's 'Formatting Guide'. If you do this, then your book is going to be designed in a manner that Amazon refers to as 'Kindle Format 8'.

So the first thing you need to do is take your content and then dump it into a Word document (ideally, your content will already be in Microsoft Word). There are other ways to make a Kindle book but this is by far the simplest and the quickest. If you don't already have Word, then it's great investment and one that's certain to be worth your while. Sign up for Office 365 and you'll also get Excel and all the other tools you associate with Office. Additionally, you'll be able to run the software on smartphones, which could come in handy if you like writing on the bus.

Now make a note of these following points, as they're kind of crucial:

File Format

The file format you're going to create your book in is DOC or DOCX. As we'll see later on, Amazon can automatically convert this for you.

However, if you want to add in guide pages etc. (see below) then you eventually want to save your file as 'Web Page, Filtered' or 'Web Page'. This should create a HTML format and it will allow Kindle to understand all of the different reference elements etc. This is easy to do in Word – you simply select that option instead of '.DOC' when 'saving as'. Just make sure that you're completely happy with the final layout and product before you go ahead.

Fonts

Word will apply paragraphs, indentations etc. by default and you can use these as you wish along with bold etc. Be careful though: if you apply a special font then it might not be supported by Kindle. Avoid downloading unique OTF files – tempting though it might be!

Images

Images must be JPEG format and they should be inserted in the center of your page. You must insert them, not copy and paste them from another source. So that means selecting Insert > Picture.

Pages

To start a new page, you can use a page break. This will normally go at the end of each chapter for instance. Note that different screen sizes make things like images a little unpredictable, so don't get too attached to a specific layout!

Adding a Table of Contents

A very useful feature to add for your book is an active table of contents. This will enable your readers to see everything that's in the book but also to jump to the relevant page simply by clicking that item on the menu.

And the great thing is that Word makes this incredibly easy. All you need to do is to use 'Heading 1' (found on the Home tab) whenever you write a chapter heading and 'Heading 2' or 'Heading 3' for your subheadings. At the end, you can then click the 'References' tab and then choose the Menu style you like.

This will now not only generate your contents but it will also be active so that people can jump anywhere in your book. Make sure that you update the table of contents every time that you update your book. Even if you're just changing the size of the font, you need to be sure that you keep the table up to date.

Bookmarks

Go to 'Insert > Bookmark' in order to add reference points in your book. Kindle will understand bookmarks called 'Start' and bookmarks called 'TOC' and that will let your readers jump to that point from anywhere in the book. These are known as **guide pages**.

Extra Pages

There are certain additional pages that you might choose to add to your book and that are fairly common to find in books you'll download from the Kindle store.

These include:

- A title page – A centered title with your sub-title and your name (or the author's name if you are not they)

- A copyright page – Include any copyright or legal notices here. Note that you automatically own copyright to anything that you create yourself. If you are commissioning the work, then you need to ensure that it is specifically stated that you will own the full copyright to the text once it is completed.

- Dedication – This is up to you but can be a nice touch that adds professionalism.

- Preface – This usually goes just after your dedication.

- Prologue – A little introduction that is normally inserted just after the preface.

- Bibliographies

- Appendices

- Notes

- Glossaries

You can also choose to include adverts for your *other* books in the back pages. This is a particularly effective way to gain more sales for those titles and allows success in one area to blead into success in others.

A very handy tool for those creating ebooks is the *Kindle Previewer* which you can find here (http://www.amazon.com/gp/feature.html?docId=1000765261). This will allow you to install a tool on your PC or Mac that will let you preview how your book is going to look and function.

Note that creating a textbook might require some more advanced formatting features. In that case, you can use the Kindle Textbook Creator (http://www.amazon.com/gp /feature.html?docId=1002998671). This is another free tool and also comes with an in-built previewer. It's currently in beta however.

CHAPTER 6

PUBLISHING YOUR BOOK

Now you have your perfectly optimized book for Kindle, the next stage is to upload it for Kindle. Yep, that's the bit you've probably been waiting for!

To get started, you just need to head over to KDP.amazon.com (http://kdp.amazon.com). This stands for 'Kindle Direct Publishing' and is where you can upload and manage your different titles.

Now you just need to sign up/log in. You can use your usual Amazon account for this and the great news is that it's *completely* free. Amazon will take a commission for the sales of your book but there is no fee for setting up in the first place, which is great news if you don't have a ton of cash to invest!

Next, you just click 'Create New Title'

From here, you then enter your title (duh) and a few extra pieces of information, such as:

- the book name
- subtitle
- series title
- volume number
- edition number
- language
- author
- publisher
- contributors
- ISBN (if you've purchased one)
- categories
- publishing rights (don't check that your book is in the public domain or you will waiver your copyright!)

Creating Your Listing and Cover Image for Maximum Sales

Creating Your Listing and Cover Image for Maximum Sales

Most of this is self-explanatory. Note though that some of these elements are going to have a big impact on how easily discoverable your book is. The description for instance is particularly important for helping people find your book and for maximizing your sales. Make sure to use your key phrases a couple of times (very subtly and only if it reads naturally) and to sell what makes your book such a good buy. Remember, we discussed earlier how mentioning similar titles is no bad thing. Likewise, you'll recall that focussing on the 'problem' that your book solves can help, as can looking at the value proposition – how your book will make someone's life better. Likewise, you need to carefully choose your category. You can select up to 2 browse categories, meaning your book will come up when people search in those areas.

There are also a few other things to select – such as an age and reading age – but these are optional.

Now move onto the next step, which is to upload and preview your book content. Once you've taken a look and you're happy with the way it looks, you'll need to confirm your content rights.

This is also the point at which you'll be adding your cover. This is one of the most important factors when it comes to getting downloads as it's going to be what people look at along with the title and description when making their decision. This is also how you will stand out when people are browsing through different options. Make sure that your book has a title that looks good in black and white (think high contrast) and choose something that immediately communicates with the readers what your book is about. It needs to look good in color too of course – as people will browse on their Kindle Fires and through their PC browsers.

Again, if you don't have the necessary skills to create a beautiful, high definition book cover – outsource it!

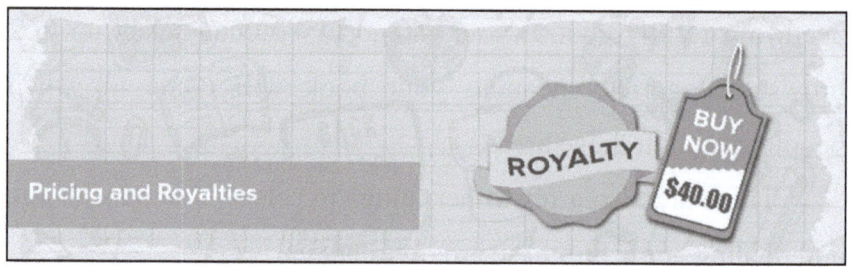

Pricing and Royalties

Finally, you need to enter your pricing and your royalties. Interestingly, you can choose to select 35% or 70% for your royalties – though the thing to keep in mind is that you can't choose 70% royalty above a certain price.

Another reason that you may choose the 35% option is that the amount you'll earn will never change. If Amazon introduces a special offer to promote its books, it will still pay you 35% of the original price you chose. On the other hand, if you opted for the 70% royalty option and Amazon has a special offer running, you'll only get 70% of the current price at that time.

Choosing your price carefully is an important part of this whole process as it will impact on your turnover and your profit margins. If you're unsure how to go ahead, Kindle actually offers some support with its KDP Pricing Support service (https://kdp.amazon.com/help?topicId=A22DBITFA52H1S). This can help you to identify how changing your price will impact on profits and sales. This takes into account factors such as your category, customer reviews and ratings, the book's best seller rank, your previous sales as an author, page count etc.

Another strategy is to compare yourself with other books in the same category. How are they priced? Which ones sell best? Ultimately, it's worth experimenting in this area and bear in mind that you can change your price whenever you like.

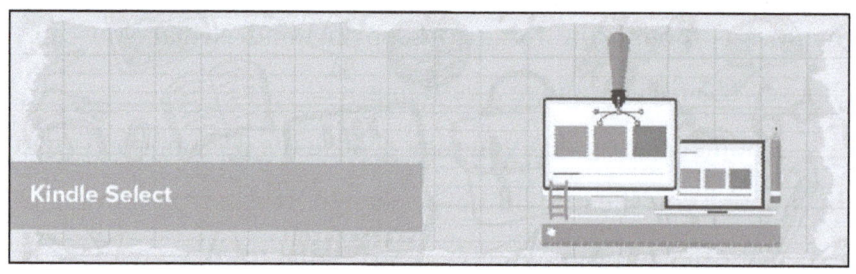

Kindle Select

There are more options too for how you want to monetize and distribute your book. You can enrol in Kindle Select for instance, in which case your book will be entered into Kindle Unlimited and will be available for Kindle Owners' Lending Library. In these cases, you will receive different royalties depending on various factors. As a rule, you'll be paid a very small amount of money each time someone reads one of your pages. The hope is that this will add up for you over time.

The big restriction? To be eligible for Kindle Direct, your book neds to be exclusive to Amazon and you can't sell it anywhere else. Conversely, if you become a best seller, you might be chosen for Select without having to agree to exclusivity. If you're a really big player, you can even negotiate different agreements for Kindle Unlimited, though most people reading this won't be in that position unfortunately.

If your book is enrolled in Kindle Select you'll also be more likely to be included in promotions – your book might even be free for a given time period. That might sound damaging (unless you opted for 35% commission) but it's actually a *very* good thing as it can increase your downloads, help you get more five star ratings and ultimately improve your position in the Kindle store. This then leads to many more sales subsequently. While there are some downsides to Kindle Select, it's ultimately going to be worth experimenting with for most people.

CHAPTER 7

MARKETING YOUR BOOK AND INCREASING YOUR RANKING AND SALES

In the process of getting to this point, we've already covered a lot of topics that should help your book to rank. You're in Kindle Select, you chose your niche well, you have a great cover and description with some keyphrases in it… so far so good. At the same time, using strict adherence to the formatting guide above will also help.

Now, what else can you do to get some exposure?

While no one knows the exact 'algorithm' that Amazon uses to define the position of its books, there are a few things that we know factor in. These are:

- Reviews
- Ratings
- Downloads

So if you have a great description and a good price, the next strategy needs to be getting as many downloads and positive reviews as you possibly can. Selling your books for a while using a low pricing is a very good way to do this, as is making sure that your books are very well written and that they'll get good reviews. Don't be afraid to ask your readers to review your book if they enjoyed it! Just as on an app, there's nothing to prevent you from including a little reminder for your readers and telling them how much it would help you out if they'd consider leaving some feedback.

If you already have a platform such as a blog or a mailing list, then this is an excellent place to promote your book and to ask people to leave positive reviews. You can also use social media etc. to promote special offers and to drive as many downloads as possible. Don't be afraid to eat into your own profits in the short term – it will help a great deal in the long term. Note as well that people are moved to write nicer reviews when they paid less for the book!

Another tip is to create an 'author page' on Amazon Central (https://authorcentral.amazon.com/gp/landing?ie=UTF8&%2AV ersion%2A=1&%2Aentries%2A=0) which will help to give your books more credibility.

You can also use other traditional forms of marketing: that means using Google AdWords for instance or Facebook ads. These might be loss leaders to begin with – meaning that you'll spend more money on advertising than you will earn – but in the long run it can help your book get more attention and more downloads which will give it the momentum you need to get into the top 20.

Likewise, you can also get your book written about in magazines and on blogs (as mentioned earlier) and especially if you're willing to offer a hefty discount for a short time. Or how about creating a video advert for YouTube? This worked very well for Tim Ferriss and his *Four Hour Chef* book.

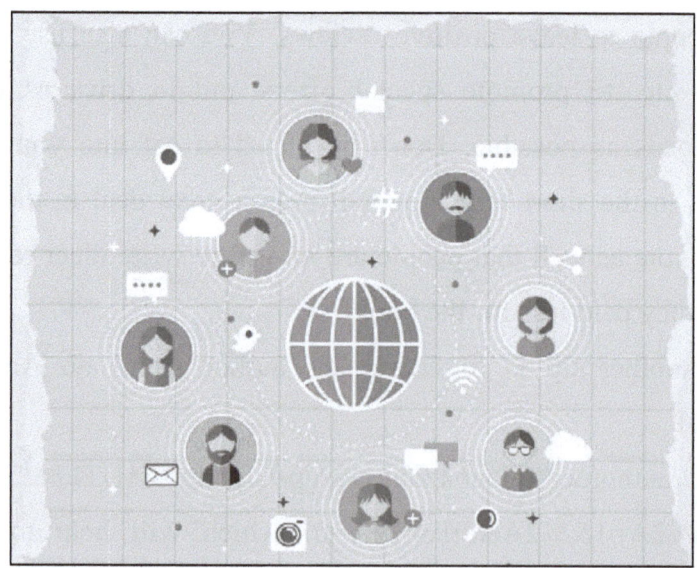

CHAPTER 8

CONCLUSIONS AND CLOSING COMMENTS

And there you have it – that's pretty much everything you need to know to start succeeding on Kindle.

To summarise what we've learned:

- Create a book in the right niche – choose a small niche but one with broad enough appeal

- Pick a niche that allows you to easily use your existing contacts to promote it

- Make sure your book is well written and edited and that it offers something genuinely new for your audience

- Outsource the creation of your book if necessary

- Think of ways to reuse content and to get maximum profit for your investment

- Format your book using the strict guidelines provided by Amazon

- Create a great cover, description etc. Subtly use key phrases.

- Consider the correct pricing and whether you should enrol into Kindle Select

- Run promotions to maximize downloads, ratings and momentum

- Promote your book externally through social media, YouTube, your blog, other sites *etc.*

- Rinse and repeat!

This is an incredibly exciting and rewarding way to make money online and with the right approach and a well written book it can also be incredibly profitable and facilitate true passive income.

Everyone's got a book in them… it's time to get yours out!

Printed by Libri Plureos GmbH in Hamburg,
Germany